W9-AFS-673

KANSAS

Julie

CHILDREN'S AND PARENTS' SERVICES
PATCHOGUE-MEDFORD LIBRARY

Big Buddy BOOKS

VISIT US AT
www.abdopublishing.com

Published by ABDO Publishing Company, PO Box 398166, Minneapolis, MN 55439.

Copyright © 2013 by Abdo Consulting Group, Inc. International copyrights reserved in all countries. No part of this book may be reproduced in any form without written permission from the publisher. Big Buddy Books™ is a trademark and logo of ABDO Publishing Company.

Printed in the United States of America, North Mankato, Minnesota.
032012
092012

♻ PRINTED ON RECYCLED PAPER

Coordinating Series Editor: Rochelle Baltzer
Editor: Sarah Tieck
Contributing Editors: Megan M. Gunderson, BreAnn Rumsch, Marcia Zappa
Graphic Design: Adam Craven
Cover Photograph: *iStockphoto*: ©iStockphoto.com/PrairieArtProject.
Interior Photographs/Illustrations: *Alamy*: Michael Hudson (p. 29), Andre Jenny (p. 11), Michael Shell (p. 27); *AP Photo*: AP Photo (pp. 23, 25), The Hays Daily News, Steven Hausler (p. 19), North Wind Picture Archives via AP Images (p. 13), Charlie Riedel (p. 26), Larry W. Smith (p. 26), Orlin Wagner (p. 11); *Getty Images*: Tim Fitzharris/Minden Pictures (p. 17), Fotosearch (p. 13); *Glow Images*: Imagebroker RM (p. 27), Wolfgang Kaehler (p. 5), Purestock (p. 27), SuperStock (p. 9); *iStockphoto*: ©iStockphoto.com/danahann (p. 21), ©iStockphoto.com/eyecrave (p. 9), ©iStockphoto.com/outtakes (p. 30), ©iStockphoto.com/Savushin (p. 30); *Shutterstock*: Phillip Lange (p. 30), Steve Shoup (p. 30).

All population figures taken from the 2010 US census.

Library of Congress Cataloging-in-Publication Data

Murray, Julie, 1969-
  Kansas / Julie Murray.
     p. cm. -- (Explore the United States)
  ISBN 978-1-61783-354-0
  1. Kansas--Juvenile literature. I. Title.
  F681.3.M87 2013
  978.1--dc23
                              2012000751

Contents

ONE NATION

The United States is a **diverse** country. It has farmland, cities, coasts, and mountains. Its people come from many different backgrounds. And, its history covers more than 200 years.

Today the country includes 50 states. Kansas is one of these states. Let's learn more about Kansas and its story!

Did You Know?

Kansas became a state on January 29, 1861. It was the thirty-fourth state to join the nation.

Kansas is in the Great Plains. This dry, grassy part of the country is known for its farmland.

KANSAS UP CLOSE

Did You Know?

Washington DC is the US capital city. Puerto Rico is a US commonwealth. This means it is governed by its own people.

The United States has four main **regions**. Kansas is in the Midwest.

Kansas shares borders with four other states. Nebraska is north. Missouri is east. Oklahoma is south. And Colorado is west.

Kansas has a total area of 82,278 square miles (213,099 sq km). About 2.9 million people live there.

REGIONS OF THE UNITED STATES

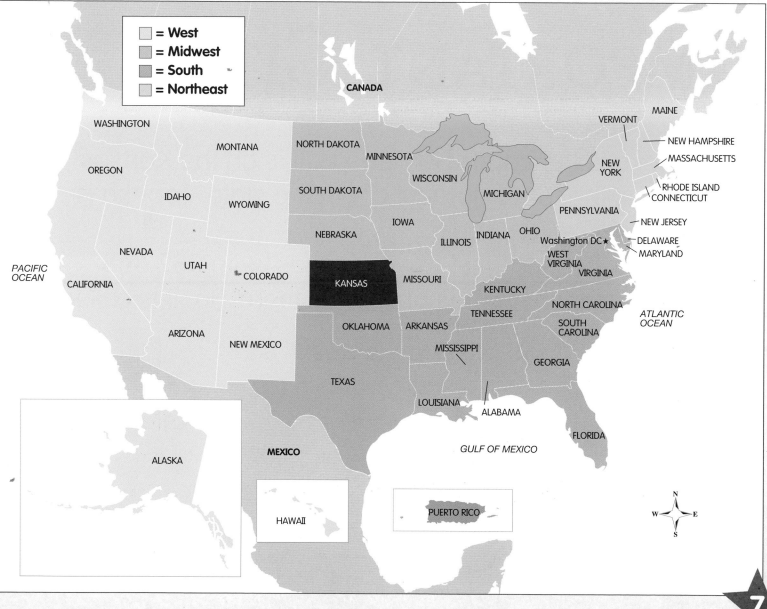

Important Cities

Topeka is the **capital** of Kansas. It is on the Kansas River. It is the fourth-largest city in the state. Topeka is home to 127,473 people.

Wichita is the largest city in Kansas, with 382,368 people. Many airplanes are made there. So, it is called "the Air Capital of the World."

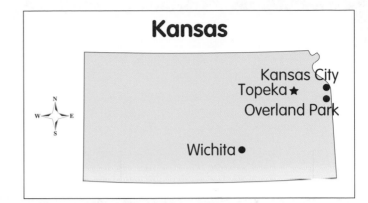

Kansas

Kansas City

Topeka ★

Overland Park

Wichita ●

The Kansas State Capitol was mostly built in the 1800s. In 2002, a statue of a Native American warrior was placed on top of the dome.

Wichita is located where the Arkansas and Little Arkansas Rivers meet.

Overland Park is the second-largest city in Kansas. It has 173,372 people. Kansas City is the state's third-largest city. Its population is 145,786. Both cities are part of the same **metropolitan** area as Kansas City, Missouri.

The Kansas Speedway in Kansas City hosts car races.

The National Agricultural Center and Hall of Fame is located near Kansas City. It honors farmers.

Kansas in History

The history of Kansas includes Native Americans, settlers, and cowboys. Native Americans were the first people to live in what is now Kansas. In 1803, the land became part of the United States in the **Louisiana Purchase**. Later, more people settled there.

Before the **American Civil War**, Northerners and Southerners fought to control Kansas. It became a state in 1861. In the late 1800s, many cowboys lived and worked in the area.

Cowboys often moved cattle from Texas to Kansas. These trips were called cattle drives.

In the late 1800s, Abilene and Dodge City (*above*) were called cow towns. They were known for cowboys and outlaws.

13

Timeline

1887

1935

1861

Susanna Madora Salter became Argonia's mayor. She was the first female mayor in the United States.

On April 14, a major dust storm ruined homes and crops. Afterward, that date was known as Black Sunday.

Kansas became the thirty-fourth state on January 29.

1800s

Kansas joined the Northern states to fight in the **American Civil War**.

University of Kansas scientists found helium in natural gas. This has many uses, including helping balloons float!

Wichita's first airplane factory was built.

1861

1919

1905

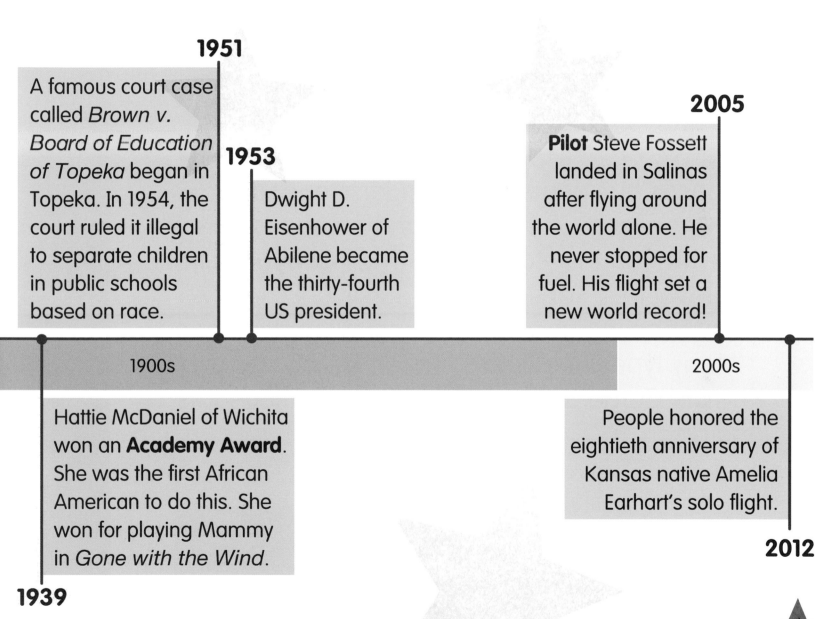

1951

A famous court case called *Brown v. Board of Education of Topeka* began in Topeka. In 1954, the court ruled it illegal to separate children in public schools based on race.

1953

Dwight D. Eisenhower of Abilene became the thirty-fourth US president.

2005

Pilot Steve Fossett landed in Salinas after flying around the world alone. He never stopped for fuel. His flight set a new world record!

1900s

2000s

Hattie McDaniel of Wichita won an **Academy Award**. She was the first African American to do this. She won for playing Mammy in *Gone with the Wind*.

People honored the eightieth anniversary of Kansas native Amelia Earhart's solo flight.

1939

2012

ACROSS THE LAND

Kansas has gentle hills, rich farmland, and flat, open land. The Kansas and Arkansas Rivers flow through the state. Horse Thief **Canyon** is in southwestern Kansas. Some say it looks like the Grand Canyon because of its colors and shapes.

Many types of animals make their homes in Kansas. Some of these include quail, pheasants, and bison.

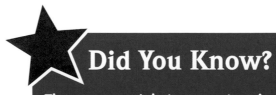

Did You Know?

The average July temperature in Kansas is 78°F (26°C). The average January temperature is 30°F (-1°C).

Kansas has many types of grasses
and wildflowers, such as sunflowers.

Tornado Alley

Kansas is located in an area called Tornado Alley. This part of the country is known for having many tornadoes.

A tornado is a spinning, twisting funnel of air. It may last for just a few minutes. Some have winds as fast as 300 miles (480 km) per hour! They are very powerful and can tear apart towns.

Did You Know?

Tornado Alley also includes Oklahoma, Texas, and Nebraska.

Tornadoes are common in the flat grasslands of Kansas.

Earning a Living

Major businesses in Kansas include farming and manufacturing. The state's most important crop is wheat. Kansas factories make airplanes, automobiles, and other products.

Many people in Kansas have service jobs. These include working for finance companies and restaurants. Other people work for the US military. Fort Leavenworth, Fort Riley, and McConnell Air Force Base are located in Kansas.

Did You Know?

Mines in Kansas produce coal, cement, and chalk.

After wheat is removed from fields, it is made into flour. Flour is used in noodles, cookies, breads, and many other foods!

HOMETOWN HEROES

Many famous people have lived in Kansas. Dwight D. Eisenhower was born in Texas in 1890. But, he grew up in Abilene. He was the US president from 1953 to 1961.

Before Eisenhower was president, he was a well-known military leader. He led the US Army during **World War II**. As president, he worked to make things fair for Americans of all races. He also started US space programs.

Eisenhower and his wife, Mamie, attended events all over the world. But, they stayed connected to Kansas. Both were buried in Abilene.

Amelia Earhart was born in Atchison in 1897. She was a famous airplane **pilot**. In 1932, she became the first woman to fly alone across the Atlantic Ocean.

In 1937, Earhart began a flight around the world. She traveled about 20,000 miles (32,000 km). Then, she disappeared! People searched for her, but she has never been found.

Earhart's family moved often during her childhood. She learned to fly around 1920 and bought her first plane in 1922.

Tour Book

Do you want to go to Kansas? If you visit the state, here are some places to go and things to do!

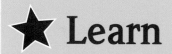

★ Taste

Have a slice of Pizza Hut pizza in Wichita. Brothers Dan and Frank Carney opened the first Pizza Hut there in 1958.

★ Learn

See more than 30 aircraft at the Combat Air Museum in Topeka. Some are from the mid-1900s!

★ Walk

Explore the Tallgrass Prairie National Preserve in the Flint Hills area of Kansas. There, you can see prairies like those that once covered much of the country.

★ Discover

The Wizard of Oz is a book and movie about a girl from Kansas. Visit Seward County Historical Museum in Liberal. There, you can see a copy of Dorothy's house from the movie.

★ Remember

Walk around the Old Cowtown Museum in Wichita. There, you can see what life was like in Kansas cow towns in the 1870s. Take a wagon ride, or drink a sarsaparilla soda!

A GREAT STATE

The story of Kansas is important to the United States. The people and places that make up this state offer something special to the country. Together with all the states, Kansas helps make the United States great.

The center of the lower 48 states is near Lebanon, Kansas. It is marked with a flag.

Fast Facts

Date of Statehood:
January 29, 1861

Population (rank):
2,853,118
(33rd most-populated state)

Total Area (rank):
82,278 square miles
(15th largest state)

Motto:
"Ad Astra Per Aspera" (To the
Stars Through Difficulties)

Nickname:
Sunflower State,
Jayhawker State

State Capital:
Topeka

Flag:

Flower: Common Sunflower

Postal Abbreviation:
KS

Tree: Eastern Cottonwood

Bird: Western Meadowlark

Important Words

Academy Award an award given by the Academy of Motion Picture Arts and Sciences to the best actors and filmmakers of the year.

American Civil War the war between the Northern and Southern states from 1861 to 1865.

canyon a long, narrow valley between two cliffs.

capital a city where government leaders meet.

diverse made up of things that are different from each other.

Louisiana Purchase land the United States purchased from France in 1803. It extended from the Mississippi River to the Rocky Mountains and from Canada through the Gulf of Mexico.

metropolitan of or relating to a large city, usually with nearby smaller cities called suburbs.

pilot someone whose job is to direct a ship, an airplane, or a spacecraft.

region a large part of a country that is different from other parts.

World War II a war fought in Europe, Asia, and Africa from 1939 to 1945.

Web Sites

To learn more about Kansas, visit ABDO Publishing Company online. Web sites about Kansas are featured on our Book Links page. These links are routinely monitored and updated to provide the most current information available.

www.abdopublishing.com

Index

DISCARD

JUN 05 2013